Colors of
ISRAEL

by Laurie M. Grossman
illustrations by Helen Byers

Carolrhoda Books, Inc. / Minneapolis

In loving memory of my grandmother, Lola Koper Bach, who helped raise me, and in memory of her family, who perished in the Holocaust, never to see the colors of Israel: Rivka, Levi, Fayge, Rahmiel, Yehiel, and Bayla —LMG

These illustrations are dedicated to the memory of my father, Laurence P. Byers, and my mother, Muriel A. Byers Peterson, who both knew Israel and prayed for peace. —HB

Special thanks to Professor Rex Honey of the Global Studies Program at the University of Iowa and Professors Caesar Farah and Hisham Khalek of Middle Eastern and Islamic Studies at the University of Minnesota for their assistance with the preparation of this book.

Text copyright © 2002 by Laurie M. Grossman
Illustrations copyright © 2002 by Helen Byers

This book is available in two editions:
Library binding by Carolrhoda Books, Inc.,
a division of Lerner Publishing Group
Soft cover by First Avenue Editions,
an imprint of Lerner Publishing Group
241 First Avenue North, Minneapolis, MN 55401 U.S.A.

Website address: www.lernerbooks.com

Library of Congress Cataloging-in-Publication Data

Grossman, Laurie M.
    Colors of Israel / by Laurie M. Grossman; illustrations by Helen Byers.
      p. cm. — (Colors of the world)
    Includes index.
    Summary: Explores the different colors found in Israel's history, culture, and landscape.
      ISBN 1-57505-382-9 (lib. bdg: alk paper)
      ISBN 1-57505-523-6 (pbk.: alk. paper)
      1. Israel—Juvenile literature. 2. Colors, Words for—Juvenile literature.
    [1. Israel. 2. Color.] I. Byers, Helen, ill. II. Title. III. Series.
    DS118.G8853 2002
    956.94—dc21   99-31802

Manufactured in the United States of America
1 2 3 4 5 6 – JR – 07 06 05 04 03 02

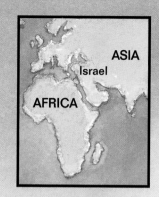

Introduction

Israel is a country of ancient history and rich tradition. Three major religions—Islam, Christianity, and Judaism—trace their beliefs back to Israel. Powerful nations have fought over this land for thousands of years. Israel is only about the size of New Jersey and is located in southwestern Asia, or the Middle East. It is the meeting point of Africa, Asia, and Europe.

Israel has large deserts and many farming villages. But most Israelis live in crowded cities near the Mediterranean Sea and in Israel's capital, Jerusalem. In 1948, Israel, a homeland for Jews all over the world, became a state. Most of the more than six million people living in Israel are Jews. But Israel is also home to more than one million Arabs. Hebrew and Arabic are Israel's two official languages.

GOLD

זהב

Za-hav
(zah-HAHV)
Hebrew

ذَهَبي

D̲ahaby
(that-HAH-bee)
Arabic

Some people call Israel's busy capital "Jerusalem of **Gold**." At sunset the city's many stone buildings glow golden. Jerusalem is sacred to three religions—Islam, Judaism, and Christianity. An ancient shrine with a shiny gold dome stands on a low hill in Jerusalem. This Islamic shrine, called the Dome of the Rock, is one of the city's most important landmarks. Followers of the Islamic religion believe that their prophet Muhammad rose to heaven at the spot where the shrine stands.

Below the shrine is the ancient Western Wall. The Wall once surrounded part of the holy Jewish Temple, which stood where the shrine stands. The Temple was destroyed nearly two thousand years ago. People come to pray at the Wall and stuff scraps of paper covered with prayers into its cracks. Jewish children wearing gold paper crowns receive their first prayer books at this historic spot. Christians also visit Jerusalem of Gold, where Jesus preached and died.

5

6

אדום   RED   أَحمَر

Adom
(ah-DOHM)
Hebrew

Aḥmar
(AH-mar)
Arabic

In an Israeli Arab wedding ceremony, the bride might wear a traditional black gown embroidered with **red** thread. It is also traditional for a newly married couple to live near the groom's family. Several generations of parents and their grown children often share a courtyard or live close to each other in the same town. This group of families living near each other is called a *hamula* (hah-MOO-lah). During times of celebration, the hamula comes together to share a meal, drink strong coffee, and listen to music. Someone strums the *auod* (ood), a wooden instrument like a guitar, while everyone sings love ballads and folk songs.

שחור BLACK أَسوَد

Shakhor
(shah-HOHR)
Hebrew

Aswad
(AHS-wahd)
Arabic

Visitors to the Dead Sea coat themselves with **black** mud that oozes at the shore. They let the thick, smooth mud dry before washing it off. Some people believe it is good for their skin. Many tourists relax in mud baths along the shore and buy bags of Dead Sea mud to take home with them. Other people dig up mud themselves from under the rocky sand.

The Dead Sea is not really a sea—it's a lake, and it's the saltiest body of water in the world. It is called the "Dead Sea" because it's too salty for plants or fish to live in. Israeli companies use the Dead Sea's minerals to make table salt and fertilizers. Tourists come to dip in the crystal blue water, but the salt makes it hard to swim. If you jump into the Dead Sea, you will float to the top!

צהוב   YELLOW   أَصفَر

Tsahov
(tzah-HOHV)
Hebrew

Aṣfar
(AHS-far)
Arabic

A **yellow** robot moves toward a backpack that has been left alone on the sidewalk. Israeli police officers block off traffic and stop people from coming near. Then they use a remote control to direct the yellow robot to shake the bag. The police officers must be very careful because the bag could contain a bomb. They might direct the robot to blow up the bag, especially if they aren't sure what's inside.

Different national groups disagree about who should be living in Israel. Some people, called terrorists, believe that frightening citizens is a way to bring about change. Terrorists use bombs as one way to frighten people. They might hide a bomb in an empty bag or container, such as a backpack or a garbage can. If a bomb is not discovered in time, it explodes and can hurt or kill people. Most people want to stop terrorism. They are working to make Israel a safer place, where different groups can live together in peace.

11

כחול   BLUE   أَزْرَق

Kakhol
(kah-HOHL)
Hebrew

Azraq
(AHZ-rahk)
Arabic

B'nai Akiva (b'nay ah-KEE-vah) youth group members wear **blue** kerchiefs and shirts with blue lacing. Each week, thousands of Israeli boys and girls go to different youth groups to participate in activities with other children. B'nai Akiva is one of the most popular youth movements in Israel. The blue and white in the B'nai Akiva uniform match the colors in Israel's flag. Blue and white were chosen as the national colors because they are found in traditional prayer shawls called *tallith* (tah-LEET). Jewish men have worn the white tallith with blue threading for thousands of years.

In B'nai Akiva, children celebrate Israeli culture. They often discuss Israeli values, such as the welcoming of immigrants and the settling of land. To get ready for a big youth group weekend, they paint murals and create displays that express these and other important Israeli values. Children also learn Israeli songs, and they march and carry bright torches as they sing. Playing ball games and camping in Israel's countryside are other favorite activities.

13

חום בהיר   TAN   أَسمَر

Khoom baheer
(hoom bah-HEER)
Hebrew

Asmar
(AHS-mar)
Arabic

Tan wild goats called ibex live in Israel's rocky deserts, which cover more than half of the country. Ibex have an easier time living in the hot, dry desert than people do. They need less water than humans do, and their shiny tan coats keep them cool by reflecting the sun's heat. Their tan coloring also helps ibex hide from enemies because it allows them to blend with the desert rocks. The goats spend much of their lives on steep desert cliffs. To get around, they nimbly jump from rock to rock. Their Hebrew name, *yael* (yah-EL), means "going up." Jews use the thick, curled horns of the ibex to make a musical instrument called the *shofar* (shoh-FAR). The blast from a shofar can sound like a sheep bleating or a baby crying. Jewish Israelis blow these horns each autumn when they welcome their new year.

14

15

ורוד　　PINK　　زهري

Varod
(vah-ROHD)
Hebrew

Zahry
(ZAH-hree)
Arabic

All year long, Israeli children gulp down gallons of a **pink** raspberry-flavored soda water called *petel* (PEH-tehl). Many families have a special soda maker right in their kitchen. Children drink petel with lunch, the biggest meal of the day. Common main dishes are soy patties and breaded chicken patties. Israelis also eat lots of dairy food. They especially love soft white cheeses. But most Jewish Israelis do not eat meat with milk products. Jewish religious law states that Jews must not eat dairy foods and meat together. Other foods such as fruits, vegetables, nuts, and breads can be eaten with either dairy products or meat. So Israeli children can drink raspberry petel with any kind of meal!

לבן WHITE أَبْيَض

Lavan
(lah-VAHN)
Hebrew

Abyaḍ
(AHB-yahd)
Arabic

Every Saturday, many Jewish Israelis wear festive **white** clothes in honor of the Jewish Sabbath. The Sabbath is a holy day for the Jewish people. Each week it begins at sundown on Friday and ends at sundown on Saturday. During this time, many shops close, and most buses stop running.

For some Israelis, the Sabbath is a special time of prayer. People walk to their nearby synagogue, and men and boys wear bright white shirts and prayer shawls. It is traditional for men and women to pray separately in Israeli synagogues. But some synagogues are beginning to have religious services with men and women together. The Sabbath is also a time for families to be together. Many families prepare special meals and invite guests to their homes to eat and sing. Saturday is a day for relaxation and enjoyment. Israelis go to the beach with friends or gather together for sing-alongs. Everyone from small children to grandparents joins in the fun.

כתום   ORANGE   بُرتُقالي

Katom
(kah-TOHM)
Hebrew

Burtuqāly
(boor-too-KAH-lee)
Arabic

Many **orange**-colored fruits, such as tangerines, oranges, mangoes, apricots, nectarines, and dates, are grown in Israel. Israel's most important crops are citrus fruits—especially oranges. Only small portions of land in western and northern Israel receive enough rain to grow crops. In desert areas, farmers use pipes to drip fresh water and fertilizer at the roots of crops planted in the dry sand.

Some of the farms in Israel are run by a kind of community called a *kibbutz* (kee-BUHTS), which means "gathering." On a kibbutz, families live and work together. Many daily chores, such as washing laundry, are done as a community. People gather in a dining hall for most meals. Older children and adults take turns serving the meals and clearing the tables. Families live in separate homes, but they share other necessities, such as cars. Earnings from the kibbutz farms or factories are also shared equally.

20

21

GREEN

ירוק

Yahrok
(yah-ROHK)
Hebrew

أَخضَر

Akhḍar
(AHKH-dahr)
Arabic

If you were a visitor to a traditional Israeli Arab home, you might notice **green** steps or a green door leading into the house. This is a sign of welcome. Inside the home, the living room might have green windowsills, walls, and furniture. You might see sofa cushions, tablecloths, and bedspreads embroidered with green plants, flowers, and trees. Even serving trays are sometimes woven from straw that has been dyed green. Green is a meaningful color in Arab culture. It represents Islam, the religion followed by most Israeli Arabs. In Islam, green symbolizes life, rebirth, and the importance of fertile land. For Israeli Arabs, the color also represents the olive tree, which has leaves that stay green all year round. Traditional Israeli Arab life has long centered around the harvesting of this honored tree.

23

Index